50 Zero Waste Cooking Recipes for Home

By: Kelly Johnson

Table of Contents

- Vegetable Scraps Broth
- Potato Peel Chips
- Citrus Zest Marmalade
- Stale Bread Pudding
- Carrot Top Pesto
- Broccoli Stem Slaw
- Pickled Vegetable Scraps
- Banana Peel Smoothie
- Herb Stem Chimichurri
- Radish Greens Salad
- Eggshell Fertilizer for Plants
- Cauliflower Leaves Stir-Fry
- Apple Core Jelly
- Tomato Water Vinaigrette
- Rice Water for Cooking
- Pumpkin Seed Granola
- Fruit Peel Infused Water
- Zucchini Flower Fritters
- Sweet Potato Vine Chips
- Beet Greens Quiche
- Overripe Fruit Ice Cream
- Coffee Ground Cookies
- Corn Cob Chowder
- Beetroot Stem Stir-Fry
- Leftover Rice Frittata
- Avocado Pit Smoothie
- Cabbage Core Sauerkraut
- Herb Stem Tea
- Pickled Garlic Scapes
- Strawberry Tops Smoothie
- Broccoli Leaf Chips
- Squash Blossom Tacos

- Melon Rind Pickles
- Cucumber Peel Salad
- Grapefruit Zest Vinaigrette
- Potato Water Pancakes
- Leftover Veggie Stir-Fry
- Fruit Scrap Muffins
- Herb Oil from Stems
- Sweet Potato Skin Mash
- Cabbage Stalk Coleslaw
- Watermelon Rind Salad
- Onion Skin Broth
- Leftover Salad Wraps
- Almond Pulp Cookies
- Shrimp Shell Stock
- Radish Top Soup
- Dried Herb Sachets from Stems
- Lemon Pulp Dressing
- Spent Grain Bread

Vegetable Scraps Broth
Ingredients:

- Vegetable scraps (onion peels, carrot tops, celery leaves, etc.)
- 10 cups water
- 1 bay leaf
- 1 teaspoon black peppercorns
- Salt to taste

Instructions:

1. **Combine Ingredients:** Place all vegetable scraps in a large pot. Add water, bay leaf, peppercorns, and salt.
2. **Simmer:** Bring to a boil, then reduce heat and let simmer for 45 minutes to 1 hour.
3. **Strain:** Remove from heat and strain the broth through a fine-mesh sieve. Discard solids.
4. **Store:** Use immediately or store in the refrigerator for up to a week or freeze for later use.

Potato Peel Chips
Ingredients:

- Potato peels (from 2-3 potatoes)
- Olive oil
- Salt and pepper
- Optional seasonings (paprika, garlic powder, etc.)

Instructions:

1. **Preheat Oven:** Preheat the oven to 400°F (200°C).
2. **Prepare Peels:** Rinse potato peels and pat them dry.
3. **Season:** Toss with olive oil, salt, pepper, and any additional seasonings.
4. **Bake:** Spread peels on a baking sheet in a single layer and bake for 15-20 minutes until crispy.
5. **Serve:** Let cool slightly before serving.

Citrus Zest Marmalade
Ingredients:

- Zest from 2 oranges and 2 lemons
- 2 cups sugar
- 2 cups water
- Juice from zested oranges and lemons

Instructions:

1. **Prepare Ingredients:** In a pot, combine citrus zest, sugar, water, and citrus juice.
2. **Cook:** Bring to a boil, then reduce heat and simmer for 30-40 minutes until thickened.
3. **Jar:** Pour into sterilized jars and let cool. Store in the refrigerator.
4. **Serve:** Use as a spread or topping.

Stale Bread Pudding
Ingredients:

- 4 cups stale bread, cubed
- 2 cups milk
- 3 eggs
- 1 cup sugar
- 1 teaspoon vanilla extract
- 1 teaspoon cinnamon
- Optional: raisins or chocolate chips

Instructions:

1. **Preheat Oven:** Preheat the oven to 350°F (175°C).
2. **Combine Ingredients:** In a bowl, whisk together milk, eggs, sugar, vanilla, and cinnamon.
3. **Mix Bread:** Place stale bread in a greased baking dish and pour the milk mixture over it. Add raisins or chocolate chips if desired.
4. **Bake:** Bake for 30-40 minutes until set and golden.
5. **Serve:** Let cool slightly before serving, warm or at room temperature.

Carrot Top Pesto
Ingredients:

- 1 cup carrot tops, washed and chopped
- 1/2 cup nuts (pine nuts, walnuts, or almonds)
- 1/2 cup grated Parmesan cheese
- 2 cloves garlic
- 1/2 cup olive oil
- Salt and pepper to taste

Instructions:

1. **Blend Ingredients:** In a food processor, combine carrot tops, nuts, Parmesan, garlic, salt, and pepper.
2. **Add Olive Oil:** With the processor running, slowly add olive oil until the mixture is smooth.
3. **Serve:** Use immediately on pasta, sandwiches, or as a dip, or store in the refrigerator for up to a week.

Broccoli Stem Slaw
Ingredients:

- 2 broccoli stems, peeled and shredded
- 1 carrot, grated
- 1/4 cup red onion, thinly sliced
- 1/4 cup mayonnaise
- 1 tablespoon apple cider vinegar
- Salt and pepper to taste

Instructions:

1. **Mix Vegetables:** In a bowl, combine shredded broccoli stems, grated carrot, and red onion.
2. **Make Dressing:** In a separate bowl, whisk together mayonnaise, apple cider vinegar, salt, and pepper.
3. **Combine:** Pour dressing over vegetables and toss to combine.
4. **Chill and Serve:** Let sit in the refrigerator for 30 minutes before serving.

Pickled Vegetable Scraps
Ingredients:

- Vegetable scraps (carrot peels, cucumber ends, onion skins, etc.)
- 1 cup vinegar (white or apple cider)
- 1 cup water
- 1 tablespoon salt
- 1 tablespoon sugar
- Optional spices (mustard seeds, dill, garlic)

Instructions:

1. **Prepare Brine:** In a saucepan, combine vinegar, water, salt, sugar, and any optional spices. Bring to a boil.
2. **Pack Scraps:** Place vegetable scraps in a clean jar.
3. **Add Brine:** Pour hot brine over the scraps, ensuring they are fully submerged.
4. **Cool and Refrigerate:** Let cool, then seal and refrigerate for at least 24 hours before using. Store in the refrigerator for up to a month.

Banana Peel Smoothie
Ingredients:

- 1 banana peel, cleaned and chopped
- 1 banana
- 1 cup spinach or kale
- 1 cup almond milk (or any milk of choice)
- 1 tablespoon peanut butter (optional)
- Ice cubes (optional)

Instructions:

1. **Prepare Banana Peel:** Ensure the banana peel is clean. Chop it into smaller pieces.
2. **Blend Ingredients:** In a blender, combine the chopped banana peel, banana, spinach or kale, almond milk, and peanut butter.
3. **Blend Smoothly:** Blend until smooth. Add ice cubes for a chilled smoothie if desired.
4. **Serve:** Pour into a glass and enjoy!

Herb Stem Chimichurri
Ingredients:

- 1 cup mixed herb stems (parsley, cilantro, basil, etc.)
- 1/2 cup olive oil
- 1/4 cup red wine vinegar
- 2 garlic cloves, minced
- 1/2 teaspoon red pepper flakes (optional)
- Salt and pepper to taste

Instructions:

1. **Combine Ingredients:** In a bowl, mix the chopped herb stems, olive oil, red wine vinegar, minced garlic, red pepper flakes, salt, and pepper.
2. **Blend or Mix:** For a smoother texture, blend in a food processor until well combined.
3. **Chill:** Let sit in the refrigerator for at least 30 minutes to allow flavors to meld.
4. **Serve:** Use as a marinade or dressing.

Radish Greens Salad
Ingredients:

- 2 cups radish greens, washed and chopped
- 1 cup cherry tomatoes, halved
- 1/4 cup red onion, thinly sliced
- 1/4 cup feta cheese (optional)
- 2 tablespoons olive oil
- 1 tablespoon lemon juice
- Salt and pepper to taste

Instructions:

1. **Prepare Salad Base:** In a large bowl, combine radish greens, cherry tomatoes, red onion, and feta cheese.
2. **Dress Salad:** In a small bowl, whisk together olive oil, lemon juice, salt, and pepper.
3. **Combine:** Drizzle the dressing over the salad and toss gently to combine.
4. **Serve:** Enjoy fresh as a side dish or light meal.

Eggshell Fertilizer for Plants
Ingredients:

- 10-12 eggshells, cleaned and dried

Instructions:

1. **Crush Eggshells:** Crush the dried eggshells into small pieces or powder.
2. **Add to Soil:** Sprinkle the crushed eggshells into the soil of your plants.
3. **Benefits:** Eggshells provide calcium to plants, helping to strengthen their cell walls and promote healthy growth.

Cauliflower Leaves Stir-Fry
Ingredients:

- 2 cups cauliflower leaves, washed and chopped
- 1 tablespoon olive oil
- 2 garlic cloves, minced
- 1 tablespoon soy sauce
- Salt and pepper to taste
- Optional: sesame seeds for garnish

Instructions:

1. **Heat Oil:** In a large skillet, heat olive oil over medium heat.
2. **Add Garlic:** Add minced garlic and sauté for 1 minute until fragrant.
3. **Stir-Fry Leaves:** Add cauliflower leaves and stir-fry for about 5-7 minutes until tender.
4. **Season:** Add soy sauce, salt, and pepper. Stir to combine.
5. **Serve:** Garnish with sesame seeds if desired and serve warm.

Apple Core Jelly
Ingredients:

- Cores from 5-6 apples
- 4 cups water
- 1 cup sugar
- 1 tablespoon lemon juice

Instructions:

1. **Prepare Cores:** Place apple cores in a large pot with water.
2. **Simmer:** Bring to a boil and then simmer for about 30-40 minutes.
3. **Strain:** Strain the mixture through a fine mesh sieve, discarding the solids.
4. **Cook Jelly:** Return the liquid to the pot, add sugar and lemon juice, and boil until it reaches a jelly-like consistency.
5. **Jar:** Pour into sterilized jars and let cool. Store in the refrigerator.

Tomato Water Vinaigrette
Ingredients:

- 1 cup tomato water (juice strained from tomatoes)
- 1/4 cup olive oil
- 2 tablespoons red wine vinegar
- 1 teaspoon Dijon mustard
- Salt and pepper to taste

Instructions:

1. **Combine Ingredients:** In a bowl, whisk together tomato water, olive oil, red wine vinegar, and Dijon mustard.
2. **Season:** Add salt and pepper to taste.
3. **Serve:** Drizzle over salads or use as a dressing for roasted vegetables. Store in the refrigerator for up to a week.

Rice Water for Cooking
Ingredients:

- 1 cup rice (any variety)
- 4 cups water

Instructions:

1. **Rinse Rice:** Rinse the rice under cold water until the water runs clear to remove excess starch.
2. **Soak Rice:** Combine the rinsed rice and water in a bowl or pot. Let it soak for 30 minutes to an hour.
3. **Strain Water:** After soaking, strain the water into a separate container. This rice water can be used for cooking, watering plants, or as a base for soups.

Pumpkin Seed Granola
Ingredients:

- 2 cups rolled oats
- 1 cup pumpkin seeds
- 1/2 cup honey or maple syrup
- 1/4 cup coconut oil, melted
- 1 teaspoon vanilla extract
- 1/2 teaspoon cinnamon
- 1/4 teaspoon salt

Instructions:

1. **Preheat Oven:** Preheat the oven to 350°F (175°C).
2. **Mix Ingredients:** In a large bowl, combine rolled oats, pumpkin seeds, honey or maple syrup, melted coconut oil, vanilla extract, cinnamon, and salt. Mix until everything is well coated.
3. **Spread on Baking Sheet:** Spread the mixture evenly on a baking sheet lined with parchment paper.
4. **Bake:** Bake for 20-25 minutes, stirring halfway through, until golden brown.
5. **Cool and Store:** Allow to cool completely before storing in an airtight container.

Fruit Peel Infused Water
Ingredients:

- Peels from fruits (like oranges, lemons, apples, or cucumbers)
- 4 cups water

Instructions:

1. **Combine Ingredients:** Place the fruit peels in a large pitcher and add the water.
2. **Infuse:** Allow the mixture to sit in the refrigerator for at least 2 hours, or overnight for a stronger flavor.
3. **Serve:** Strain the peels out before serving. Enjoy the refreshing infused water!

Zucchini Flower Fritters
Ingredients:

- 10 zucchini flowers, cleaned and trimmed
- 1 cup all-purpose flour
- 1/2 cup grated Parmesan cheese
- 1/2 cup water
- 1 egg, beaten
- Salt and pepper to taste
- Oil for frying

Instructions:

1. **Make Batter:** In a bowl, combine flour, Parmesan cheese, water, beaten egg, salt, and pepper. Mix until smooth.
2. **Heat Oil:** Heat oil in a frying pan over medium heat.
3. **Fry Fritters:** Dip each zucchini flower in the batter and gently place it in the hot oil. Fry until golden brown on both sides, about 2-3 minutes per side.
4. **Drain and Serve:** Remove and drain on paper towels. Serve warm.

Sweet Potato Vine Chips
Ingredients:

- Leaves from sweet potato vines, washed and dried
- 1 tablespoon olive oil
- Salt to taste

Instructions:

1. **Preheat Oven:** Preheat the oven to 375°F (190°C).
2. **Toss Leaves:** In a bowl, toss sweet potato leaves with olive oil and salt.
3. **Bake:** Spread the leaves in a single layer on a baking sheet. Bake for 10-15 minutes, or until crispy.
4. **Serve:** Allow to cool and enjoy as a snack.

Beet Greens Quiche
Ingredients:

- 1 pie crust (store-bought or homemade)
- 2 cups beet greens, chopped
- 1 cup milk
- 3 eggs
- 1 cup cheese (cheddar or feta)
- Salt and pepper to taste

Instructions:

1. **Preheat Oven:** Preheat the oven to 350°F (175°C).
2. **Sauté Greens:** In a skillet, sauté beet greens until wilted, about 5 minutes.
3. **Mix Filling:** In a bowl, whisk together milk, eggs, salt, and pepper. Stir in the sautéed greens and cheese.
4. **Pour into Crust:** Pour the mixture into the pie crust.
5. **Bake:** Bake for 30-35 minutes, or until the filling is set and the top is golden.
6. **Cool and Serve:** Allow to cool slightly before slicing and serving.

Overripe Fruit Ice Cream
Ingredients:

- 4 cups overripe fruit (bananas, peaches, or any fruit of choice)
- 1/2 cup yogurt or coconut milk
- 1 tablespoon honey or maple syrup (optional)

Instructions:

1. **Prepare Fruit:** Peel and chop the overripe fruit.
2. **Blend Ingredients:** In a blender or food processor, combine the fruit, yogurt, and honey or maple syrup. Blend until smooth.
3. **Freeze:** Pour the mixture into a container and freeze for at least 4 hours or until solid.
4. **Serve:** Scoop out and serve as a refreshing dessert.

Coffee Ground Cookies
Ingredients:

- 1 cup all-purpose flour
- 1/2 cup coffee grounds
- 1/2 cup butter, softened
- 1/2 cup sugar
- 1/4 cup brown sugar
- 1 egg
- 1 teaspoon vanilla extract
- 1/2 teaspoon baking soda
- Pinch of salt

Instructions:

1. **Preheat Oven:** Preheat the oven to 350°F (175°C).
2. **Cream Butter and Sugars:** In a bowl, cream together the softened butter, sugar, and brown sugar until fluffy.
3. **Add Egg and Vanilla:** Beat in the egg and vanilla extract.
4. **Mix Dry Ingredients:** In another bowl, mix flour, coffee grounds, baking soda, and salt. Gradually add to the wet mixture, stirring until combined.
5. **Drop Cookies:** Drop spoonfuls of dough onto a baking sheet.
6. **Bake:** Bake for 10-12 minutes, or until the edges are golden.
7. **Cool and Enjoy:** Allow to cool before serving.

Corn Cob Chowder

Ingredients:

- 2 corn cobs, stripped of kernels
- 4 cups vegetable or chicken broth
- 1 onion, chopped
- 2 potatoes, diced
- 1 cup milk or cream
- Salt and pepper to taste
- Fresh herbs for garnish (optional)

Instructions:

1. **Sauté Onions:** In a large pot, sauté the chopped onion until translucent.
2. **Add Potatoes and Broth:** Add the diced potatoes and broth to the pot. Bring to a boil and cook until the potatoes are tender.
3. **Add Corn:** Stir in the corn kernels and cook for an additional 5 minutes.
4. **Blend for Creaminess:** If desired, blend a portion of the chowder for a creamier texture, then return to the pot.
5. **Stir in Milk:** Add milk or cream, and season with salt and pepper. Heat through.
6. **Serve:** Garnish with fresh herbs if desired and enjoy.

Beetroot Stem Stir-Fry
Ingredients:

- Beetroot stems, chopped
- 2 tablespoons olive oil
- 2 cloves garlic, minced
- Salt and pepper to taste
- Lemon juice (optional)

Instructions:

1. **Heat Oil:** In a skillet, heat olive oil over medium heat.
2. **Add Garlic:** Sauté garlic until fragrant, about 1 minute.
3. **Stir-Fry Stems:** Add the chopped beetroot stems and stir-fry for 5-7 minutes until tender.
4. **Season:** Season with salt and pepper. Add lemon juice if desired before serving.

Leftover Rice Frittata
Ingredients:

- 2 cups cooked rice
- 4 eggs
- 1/2 cup cheese (optional)
- 1 cup vegetables (like bell peppers, spinach, or onions)
- Salt and pepper to taste
- Olive oil for cooking

Instructions:

1. **Preheat Oven:** Preheat the oven to 375°F (190°C).
2. **Sauté Vegetables:** In an oven-safe skillet, heat olive oil and sauté the vegetables until tender.
3. **Mix Eggs and Rice:** In a bowl, whisk together eggs, cooked rice, cheese, salt, and pepper.
4. **Combine:** Pour the egg mixture over the sautéed vegetables in the skillet.
5. **Bake:** Bake in the oven for 20-25 minutes, or until the eggs are set.
6. **Serve:** Slice and serve warm.

Avocado Pit Smoothie
Ingredients:

- 1 avocado pit, cleaned and chopped
- 1 ripe avocado
- 1 banana
- 1 cup spinach (optional)
- 2 cups almond milk or water
- Honey or maple syrup to taste (optional)

Instructions:

1. **Prepare Pit:** Peel the avocado pit and chop it into smaller pieces.
2. **Blend Ingredients:** In a blender, combine the avocado, banana, chopped pit, spinach, and almond milk. Blend until smooth.
3. **Sweeten:** Add honey or maple syrup if desired and blend again.
4. **Serve:** Pour into a glass and enjoy!

Cabbage Core Sauerkraut

Ingredients:

- Cabbage core, chopped
- 1 tablespoon salt
- Water (as needed)

Instructions:

1. **Prepare Cabbage:** Place the chopped cabbage core in a bowl.
2. **Add Salt:** Sprinkle salt over the cabbage and massage it for a few minutes until it releases moisture.
3. **Pack into Jar:** Pack the mixture tightly into a clean jar, leaving some space at the top.
4. **Add Water:** If needed, add enough water to cover the cabbage.
5. **Ferment:** Cover with a lid and leave at room temperature for 1-2 weeks, checking for taste.
6. **Store:** Once fermented to your liking, transfer to the fridge.

Herb Stem Tea
Ingredients:

- Stems from herbs (like parsley, cilantro, or basil)
- 4 cups water
- Honey or lemon (optional)

Instructions:

1. **Boil Water:** In a pot, bring water to a boil.
2. **Add Herb Stems:** Add the herb stems to the boiling water and reduce to a simmer.
3. **Steep:** Let steep for 10-15 minutes.
4. **Strain:** Strain the tea into cups. Add honey or lemon if desired before serving.

Pickled Garlic Scapes
Ingredients:

- 1 bunch garlic scapes, trimmed
- 1 cup vinegar (white or apple cider)
- 1 cup water
- 1 tablespoon salt
- Spices (like peppercorns, dill, or mustard seeds)

Instructions:

1. **Prepare Brine:** In a pot, combine vinegar, water, salt, and any spices. Bring to a boil and stir until the salt dissolves.
2. **Pack Scapes:** Place garlic scapes in a sterilized jar.
3. **Add Brine:** Pour the hot brine over the scapes, ensuring they are fully submerged.
4. **Seal and Cool:** Seal the jar and let it cool to room temperature before refrigerating.
5. **Pickle:** Let sit for at least 24 hours before enjoying.

Strawberry Tops Smoothie
Ingredients:

- Tops from 1 cup strawberries
- 1 banana
- 1 cup spinach (optional)
- 1 cup almond milk or yogurt
- Honey or maple syrup to taste (optional)

Instructions:

1. **Blend Ingredients:** In a blender, combine the strawberry tops, banana, spinach, and almond milk or yogurt.
2. **Sweeten:** Add honey or maple syrup if desired and blend until smooth.
3. **Serve:** Pour into a glass and enjoy immediately!

Broccoli Leaf Chips
Ingredients:

- 2 cups broccoli leaves, washed and dried
- 2 tablespoons olive oil
- Salt and pepper to taste

Instructions:

1. **Preheat Oven:** Preheat the oven to 350°F (175°C).
2. **Prepare Leaves:** Toss the broccoli leaves with olive oil, salt, and pepper in a bowl.
3. **Bake:** Spread the leaves on a baking sheet in a single layer. Bake for 10-15 minutes or until crispy.
4. **Cool and Serve:** Let cool before serving as a crunchy snack!

Squash Blossom Tacos
Ingredients:

- 1 cup squash blossoms, cleaned and chopped
- 1 small onion, diced
- 1 clove garlic, minced
- 1 tablespoon olive oil
- Corn tortillas
- Salt and pepper to taste
- Fresh cilantro and lime for garnish

Instructions:

1. **Sauté Vegetables:** In a skillet, heat olive oil over medium heat. Sauté onion and garlic until fragrant.
2. **Add Squash Blossoms:** Add the chopped squash blossoms and cook for 3-4 minutes. Season with salt and pepper.
3. **Assemble Tacos:** Warm the corn tortillas and fill them with the squash blossom mixture.
4. **Garnish and Serve:** Top with fresh cilantro and a squeeze of lime juice before serving.

Melon Rind Pickles
Ingredients:

- Rind from 1 melon, peeled and cut into strips
- 1 cup vinegar (white or apple cider)
- 1 cup water
- 1 cup sugar
- 1 tablespoon salt
- Spices (like cinnamon sticks, cloves, or ginger)

Instructions:

1. **Prepare Brine:** In a pot, combine vinegar, water, sugar, salt, and any spices. Bring to a boil until the sugar dissolves.
2. **Pack Rind:** Place the melon rind in sterilized jars.
3. **Add Brine:** Pour the hot brine over the melon rind, ensuring it is fully submerged.
4. **Seal and Cool:** Seal the jars and let them cool to room temperature before refrigerating.
5. **Pickle:** Let sit for at least 24 hours before enjoying.

Cucumber Peel Salad
Ingredients:

- Peels from 2 cucumbers
- 1 carrot, grated
- 1/4 cup red onion, thinly sliced
- 1/4 cup vinegar (rice or apple cider)
- 1 tablespoon olive oil
- Salt and pepper to taste
- Fresh herbs (like dill or parsley) for garnish

Instructions:

1. **Prepare Salad:** In a bowl, combine cucumber peels, grated carrot, and red onion.
2. **Dress Salad:** In a separate bowl, whisk together vinegar, olive oil, salt, and pepper.
3. **Combine:** Pour the dressing over the salad and toss to combine.
4. **Garnish and Serve:** Garnish with fresh herbs before serving.

Grapefruit Zest Vinaigrette
Ingredients:

- Zest from 1 grapefruit
- 1/4 cup grapefruit juice
- 1/4 cup olive oil
- 1 tablespoon honey or maple syrup
- Salt and pepper to taste

Instructions:

1. **Combine Ingredients:** In a jar, combine grapefruit zest, grapefruit juice, olive oil, honey, salt, and pepper.
2. **Shake Well:** Shake vigorously until well combined.
3. **Serve:** Drizzle over salads or use as a marinade.

Potato Water Pancakes
Ingredients:

- 1 cup potato water (from boiled potatoes)
- 1 cup all-purpose flour
- 1 teaspoon baking powder
- 1/2 teaspoon salt
- 1 egg (optional)
- Olive oil for cooking

Instructions:

1. **Mix Batter:** In a bowl, combine potato water, flour, baking powder, salt, and egg (if using) until smooth.
2. **Heat Skillet:** Heat a skillet over medium heat and add a little olive oil.
3. **Cook Pancakes:** Pour batter onto the skillet, cooking for 2-3 minutes on each side until golden brown.
4. **Serve:** Serve warm with your favorite toppings.

Leftover Veggie Stir-Fry
Ingredients:

- 2 cups assorted leftover vegetables (bell peppers, broccoli, carrots, etc.)
- 1 tablespoon olive oil
- 2 cloves garlic, minced
- 1 tablespoon soy sauce
- Salt and pepper to taste
- Cooked rice or quinoa for serving

Instructions:

1. **Heat Oil:** In a large skillet or wok, heat olive oil over medium-high heat.
2. **Sauté Garlic:** Add minced garlic and stir for about 30 seconds until fragrant.
3. **Add Veggies:** Add the leftover vegetables and stir-fry for 5-7 minutes, until heated through and slightly tender.
4. **Season:** Drizzle with soy sauce and season with salt and pepper. Stir to combine.
5. **Serve:** Serve over cooked rice or quinoa.

Fruit Scrap Muffins
Ingredients:

- 1 cup fruit scraps (apple cores, banana peels, etc., chopped)
- 1 cup all-purpose flour
- 1/2 cup sugar
- 1 teaspoon baking powder
- 1/2 teaspoon baking soda
- 1/4 teaspoon salt
- 1/2 cup milk (or dairy alternative)
- 1/4 cup vegetable oil
- 1 egg

Instructions:

1. **Preheat Oven:** Preheat the oven to 350°F (175°C) and line a muffin tin with paper liners.
2. **Mix Dry Ingredients:** In a bowl, combine flour, sugar, baking powder, baking soda, and salt.
3. **Mix Wet Ingredients:** In another bowl, whisk together milk, oil, and egg.
4. **Combine Mixtures:** Pour the wet ingredients into the dry ingredients and mix until just combined. Fold in the fruit scraps.
5. **Bake:** Divide the batter among muffin cups and bake for 20-25 minutes, or until a toothpick comes out clean.

Herb Oil from Stems

Ingredients:

- Stems from fresh herbs (basil, parsley, cilantro, etc.)
- 1/2 cup olive oil
- Salt and pepper to taste

Instructions:

1. **Blend:** In a blender or food processor, combine herb stems and olive oil. Blend until smooth.
2. **Strain:** Pour the mixture through a fine-mesh strainer into a bowl to remove the solid stems.
3. **Season:** Season the oil with salt and pepper to taste.
4. **Store:** Store in a jar in the refrigerator for up to a week. Use it as a drizzle over salads or grilled vegetables.

Sweet Potato Skin Mash
Ingredients:

- Skins from 2 medium sweet potatoes
- 1 tablespoon butter or olive oil
- Salt and pepper to taste
- Optional: garlic powder or herbs for flavor

Instructions:

1. **Boil Skins:** In a small pot, add the sweet potato skins and cover with water. Boil until tender, about 10 minutes.
2. **Mash:** Drain the skins and return them to the pot. Add butter or olive oil, and mash until smooth.
3. **Season:** Season with salt, pepper, and any additional flavors you desire.
4. **Serve:** Serve as a side dish or as a filling for wraps.

Cabbage Stalk Coleslaw
Ingredients:

- Stalks from 1 head of cabbage, finely sliced
- 1 carrot, grated
- 1/4 cup mayonnaise or yogurt
- 1 tablespoon apple cider vinegar
- Salt and pepper to taste
- Optional: diced apple or raisins for sweetness

Instructions:

1. **Combine Ingredients:** In a bowl, mix together the cabbage stalks, grated carrot, mayonnaise or yogurt, and apple cider vinegar.
2. **Season:** Season with salt and pepper to taste.
3. **Add Sweetness:** If desired, add diced apple or raisins for a touch of sweetness.
4. **Chill and Serve:** Let the coleslaw chill in the refrigerator for about 30 minutes before serving.

Watermelon Rind Salad
Ingredients:

- Rind from 1 watermelon, peeled and diced
- 1/2 cup diced cucumber
- 1/4 cup red onion, finely chopped
- 1/4 cup feta cheese, crumbled (optional)
- 2 tablespoons olive oil
- Juice of 1 lime
- Salt and pepper to taste
- Fresh mint for garnish

Instructions:

1. **Mix Ingredients:** In a large bowl, combine the diced watermelon rind, cucumber, red onion, and feta cheese.
2. **Dress Salad:** Drizzle with olive oil and lime juice. Season with salt and pepper.
3. **Garnish:** Toss gently to combine and garnish with fresh mint.
4. **Serve:** Serve chilled as a refreshing summer salad.

Onion Skin Broth
Ingredients:

- Skins from 2-3 onions
- 1 carrot, chopped
- 1 celery stalk, chopped
- 1-2 garlic cloves, smashed
- 8 cups water
- Salt and pepper to taste
- Fresh herbs (like thyme or parsley)

Instructions:

1. **Combine Ingredients:** In a large pot, combine onion skins, chopped carrot, celery, garlic, and water.
2. **Simmer:** Bring to a boil, then reduce heat and simmer for 30-45 minutes.
3. **Strain:** Strain the broth through a fine-mesh sieve, discarding the solids.
4. **Season:** Season with salt, pepper, and fresh herbs. Use as a base for soups or stews.

Leftover Salad Wraps
Ingredients:

- Leftover salad (greens, veggies, proteins, etc.)
- Tortilla wraps or lettuce leaves
- Hummus or dressing for spreading

Instructions:

1. **Prepare Wraps:** Lay out tortilla wraps or lettuce leaves on a clean surface.
2. **Fill:** Spread a layer of hummus or dressing, then fill with the leftover salad.
3. **Roll:** Roll tightly, securing the filling inside.
4. **Serve:** Cut in half and serve immediately as a light lunch or snack.

Almond Pulp Cookies
Ingredients:

- 1 cup almond pulp (leftover from making almond milk)
- 1/2 cup almond flour
- 1/2 cup sugar or sweetener of choice
- 1/4 cup coconut oil or butter, melted
- 1 teaspoon vanilla extract
- 1 egg (or flax egg for vegan option)
- 1/2 teaspoon baking powder
- Pinch of salt

Instructions:

1. **Preheat Oven:** Preheat your oven to 350°F (175°C) and line a baking sheet with parchment paper.
2. **Mix Ingredients:** In a bowl, mix together almond pulp, almond flour, sugar, melted coconut oil, vanilla extract, egg, baking powder, and salt until combined.
3. **Form Cookies:** Scoop spoonfuls of the mixture onto the prepared baking sheet. Flatten slightly.
4. **Bake:** Bake for 10-12 minutes until golden. Allow to cool before serving.

Shrimp Shell Stock
Ingredients:

- Shells from 1 pound of shrimp
- 1 onion, chopped
- 2 garlic cloves, smashed
- 1 carrot, chopped
- 8 cups water
- Salt and pepper to taste

Instructions:

1. **Combine Ingredients:** In a large pot, combine shrimp shells, onion, garlic, carrot, and water.
2. **Simmer:** Bring to a boil, then reduce heat and simmer for about 30 minutes.
3. **Strain:** Strain the stock through a fine-mesh sieve, discarding the solids.
4. **Season:** Season with salt and pepper. Use in seafood soups, risottos, or sauces.

Radish Top Soup
Ingredients:

- Radish tops (about 2 cups)
- 1 onion, chopped
- 2 garlic cloves, minced
- 4 cups vegetable broth
- 1 potato, peeled and diced
- Olive oil for sautéing
- Salt and pepper to taste

Instructions:

1. **Sauté Vegetables:** In a pot, heat olive oil over medium heat. Add onion and garlic, cooking until softened.
2. **Add Potato:** Add diced potato and cook for a few minutes.
3. **Add Radish Tops:** Add the radish tops and vegetable broth. Bring to a boil, then reduce heat and simmer for 15-20 minutes until the potato is tender.
4. **Blend and Serve:** Blend the soup until smooth. Season with salt and pepper, and serve warm.

Dried Herb Sachets from Stems
Ingredients:

- Stems from fresh herbs (like rosemary, thyme, or basil)
- Small muslin or cheesecloth bags
- Optional: dried lavender or chamomile

Instructions:

1. **Prepare Sachets:** Fill small muslin or cheesecloth bags with the herb stems. Add optional dried flowers for fragrance.
2. **Seal:** Tie the bags securely.
3. **Use:** Place sachets in drawers, closets, or hang in your car for a fresh herbal scent.

Lemon Pulp Dressing
Ingredients:

- Pulp from 2 lemons
- 1/4 cup olive oil
- 1 tablespoon honey or maple syrup
- Salt and pepper to taste
- Optional: herbs like dill or parsley

Instructions:

1. **Combine Ingredients:** In a bowl, whisk together lemon pulp, olive oil, honey, salt, and pepper until smooth.
2. **Add Herbs:** If using, add chopped herbs and mix well.
3. **Serve:** Drizzle over salads or roasted vegetables.

Spent Grain Bread
Ingredients:

- 1 cup spent grain (from brewing beer)
- 2 cups whole wheat flour
- 1/2 cup warm water
- 1 tablespoon honey or sugar
- 1 teaspoon salt
- 1 packet active dry yeast

Instructions:

1. **Activate Yeast:** In a bowl, mix warm water with honey and yeast. Let sit for 5 minutes until bubbly.
2. **Mix Ingredients:** In a large bowl, combine spent grain, whole wheat flour, and salt. Add the yeast mixture and stir until a dough forms.
3. **Knead:** Knead the dough on a floured surface for about 10 minutes until smooth.
4. **Rise:** Place the dough in a greased bowl, cover, and let it rise for 1 hour.
5. **Bake:** Preheat the oven to 375°F (190°C). Shape the dough into a loaf and place it in a greased pan. Bake for 30-35 minutes until golden brown.

www.ingramcontent.com/pod-product-compliance
Lightning Source LLC
LaVergne TN
LVHW081507060526
838201LV00056BA/2987